Survival Guides
You Didn't Know You Needed

SURVIVING
A ZOMBIE ATTACK

Thomas Kingsley Troupe

BLACK
RABBIT
BOOKS

Hi Jinx is published by Black Rabbit Books
P.O. Box 3263, Mankato, Minnesota, 56002.
www.blackrabbitbooks.com
Copyright © 2018 Black Rabbit Books

Marysa Storm, editor; Michael Sellner, designer;
Catherine Cates, production designer;
Omay Ayres, photo researcher

Library of Congress Cataloging-in-Publication Data
Names: Troupe, Thomas Kingsley, author.
Title: Surviving a zombie attack / by Thomas Kingsley
Troupe.
Description: Mankato, Minnesota : Black Rabbit
Books, [2018] | Series: Hi jinx. Survival guides
you didn't know you needed | Includes
bibliographical references and index.
Identifiers: LCCN 2017007270 (print) | LCCN
2017024863 (ebook) | ISBN 9781680723748
(e-book) | ISBN 9781680723441 (library binding)
Subjects: LCSH: Zombies–Juvenile humor. |
Survival–Juvenile humor.
Classification: LCC PN6231.Z65 (ebook) |
LCC PN6231.Z65 T76 2018 (print) | DDC 818/.602–dc23
LC record available at https://lccn.loc.gov/2017007270

Printed in China. 9/17

Image Credits

CONTENTS

Dear Reader,

To be honest, the author's **manuscript** wasn't supposed to become a book. There was a horrible mix up. You can keep reading, if you want. Just don't take any of these suggestions seriously.

Sincerely,
a very sorry editor

Chapter 1
A PLEASANT MEAL GONE WRONG

Imagine a nice, calm evening at home. You're enjoying a lovely meal with the family. Maybe you're eating a delicious burger or a fresh salad. Sounds like a perfect night.

But what if there's a groan in the distance? The sound of something creeping toward you? The stink of rotting **flesh** in the air? Oh no! It's zombies. The dead have risen from their graves. And they're hungry for brains!

Time to Survive!

The zombies are outside. They ate Mr. Sullivan next door. In no time, they'll smell you. Then they'll head your way!

Good thing you're prepared.
You've got a survival guide you never
thought you'd need. It's time to survive
a zombie attack!*

The average American eats about 15.5 pounds (7 kilograms) of pasta each year.

Survival List
Zombies' Favorite Non-Food Treats

brains

stomachs

arms

people named George

Chapter 2

FEED THE FREAKS

Believe it or not, zombies don't eat just human flesh. Some like to eat a well-prepared meal instead.* They could have told us that if their faces weren't rotten.

Did you know that zombies love eating pasta? It's squishy like brains but much tastier. Head for the kitchen. Boil up a box of spaghetti. Maybe bake some cheesy garlic bread. Zombies usually don't bite the hands that feed them!

*Editor's Note: We couldn't fact-check what zombies like. The author totally made this up.

Gum

Don't have enough time to prepare a meal? That's fine. The pressure is on when zombies come knocking. But you'll still need to keep their mouths busy.

Why not share some gum with the rotten meat bags? It'll keep their chompers off you for a while. If you're lucky, the gum might even pull their teeth out!

Where do zombies come from? Some people believe **voodoo** magic, **viruses,** or **plagues** could create zombies.

Chapter 3
FIGHT FOR YOUR LIFE

Feeding zombies won't always work. But tickling them might!

Watch out for zombie teeth, though. Stay safe by tickling them from a distance. Use a feather duster or a broom. Aim for the stomachs or armpits. They'll laugh themselves to pieces!*

Survival List
Zombies' Most Ticklish Areas

ribs
(If they're not already broken.)

stomachs
(Avoid open wounds.)

armpits
(Plug your nose.)

feet
(Hopefully, they're not wearing old shoes!)

*Editor's Note: This idea is horrible.

Bowling Balls

When possible, stay away from the walking dead. They smell bad, and they're scary. They also want to eat you. So maybe it's time to bowl!

Zombies like to walk in groups, which is perfect. They're just asking for you to throw a strike! Grab some bowling balls, wind up, and knock them down!*

*Editor's Note: What the author fails to mention is how heavy bowling balls are. Good luck running with one in your arms.

Is bowling the oldest sport ever? In the 1930s, an **archaeologist** searched an **ancient** Egyptian grave. Inside, he found **primitive** bowling balls and pins.

Chapter 4
HURRY UP AND HIDE!

Is the city full of zombies? Then it's time to move! Go somewhere you probably won't see the living dead— the graveyard!

Sure, zombies want to go where they can find food. But they don't like to eat dead brains. They like them nice and fresh. A graveyard is a great place to hide.

Survival List
Things to Pack for a Graveyard Trip

fruit snacks
board games
flashlights
books
(A book on poodles might be nice.)

17

Water Parks

Everyone knows zombies hate water. They also hate slides and climbing. So why not put some fun into your survival? Head to the nearest water park. It'll be a great place to hide!

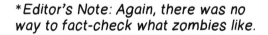

*Editor's Note: Again, there was no way to fact-check what zombies like.

You never know when zombies might attack. The walking dead are slow, clumsy, and stinky. But they're still a bit scary. Don't worry, though. This guide will keep you safe! Let the zombies snack on someone else!

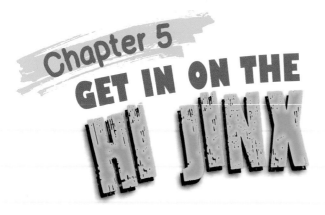

Chapter 5
GET IN ON THE HI JINX

Zombies are fun to joke about. But sometimes there are zombielike situations in real life. In 2014, a girl in the Philippines woke up at her own funeral! A relative opened her coffin and saw the girl's head move. Earlier that week, the girl had been at the hospital with a fever. Her doctor thought she was dead.

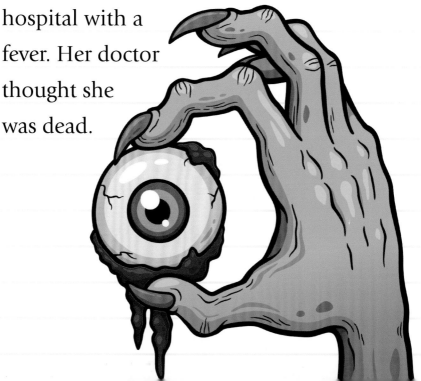

Take It One Step More

1. Zombies are popular in movies and TV shows. Why do you think that is?

2. Pretend zombies are attacking. Where would you go to escape them? Why would you choose that place?

3. What do you think the author of this book was thinking? If his suggestions are crazy, why did he write the book?

GLOSSARY

ancient (AYN-shunt)—from a time long ago

archaeologist (ahr-kee-OL-uh-jist)—someone who studies the bones, tools, and lives of ancient people

flesh (FLESH)—the soft parts of the body of an animal or person

manuscript (MAN-yuh-skript)—the original copy of a book before it has been printed

plague (PLAYG)—a disease that causes death and that spreads quickly to a large number of people

primitive (PRIM-i-tiv)—very simple and basic

virus (VAHY-ruhs)—a tiny organism that causes a disease

voodoo (VOO-doo)—a religion that is practiced mostly in the country Haiti

LEARN MORE

BOOKS

Johnson, Rebecca L. *Zombie Makers: True Stories of Nature's Undead.* Minneapolis: Millbrook Press, 2013.

Loh-Hagan, Virginia. *Zombies: Magic, Myth, and Mystery.* Magic, Myth, and Mystery. Ann Arbor, MI: Cherry Lake Publishing, 2017.

Nagle, Frances. *Zombies.* Monsters! New York: Gareth Stevens Publishing, 2017.

WEBSITES

Top Ten Facts You Need to Know about Zombies…
www.zombiefun.com/2353/top-ten-facts-you-need-to-know-about-zombies…/
Where Do Zombies Come From?
www.bbc.com/culture/story/20150828-where-do-zombies-come-from
Zombie Facts: Real and Imagined (Infographic)
www.livescience.com/16411-zombies-fact-fiction-infographic.html